**For Winnie**

**– S.G.**

**For Ada, when she was nine years old.**

**– D.S.**

**With special thanks to Professor David Norman from the Department of Earth Sciences at the University of Cambridge for his contributions and advice.**

First published 2026 by Nosy Crow Ltd
Wheat Wharf, 27a Shad Thames
London, SE1 2XZ, UK

Nosy Crow Eireann Ltd
c/o Fieldfisher Ireland LLP
45 Mespil Road, Dublin 4,
D04 W2F1, Ireland

www.nosycrow.com

ISBN 978 1 80513 555 5 (HB)
ISBN 978 1 80513 556 2 (PB)



Published in collaboration with the University of Cambridge.



A CIP catalogue record for this book is available from the British Library.

Printed in Italy following rigorous ethical sourcing standards.

1 3 5 7 9 8 6 4 2 (HB)
1 3 5 7 9 8 6 4 2 (PB)

Sedgwick Museum
*of Earth Sciences*

teeny tiny science

# I see a dinosaur

written by
**Saskia Gwinn**

illustrated by
**Daniela Sosa**


nosy crow

I see a **dinosaur**

with **four** towering legs . . .

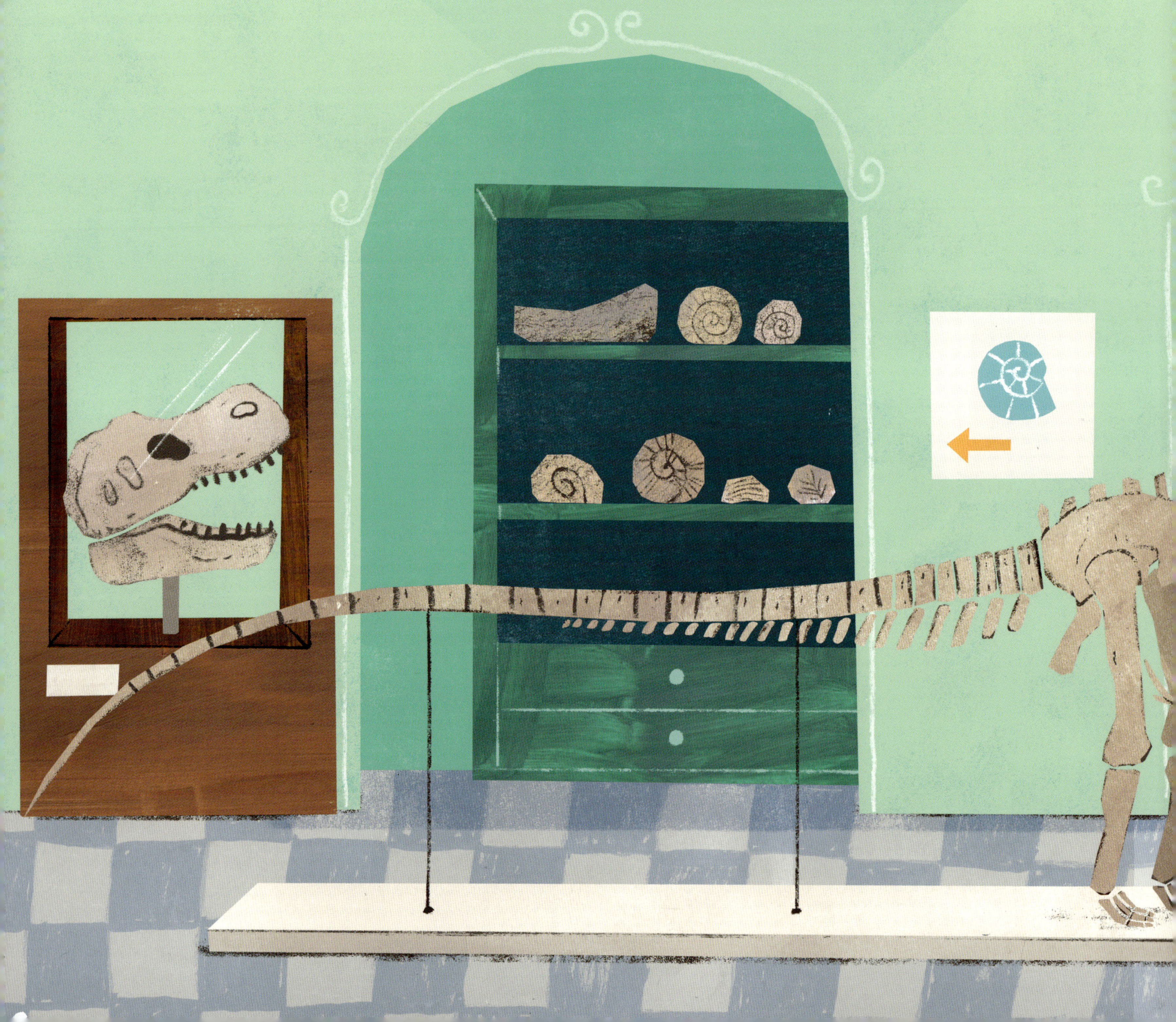

and a neck so long...

. . . it could **stretch** to the sky.

It nibbled on the leaves
on the **tallest** of trees

in the middle of a jungle
**millions** of years ago,

where it lived . . .

. . . with lots of other dinosaurs!

Dinosaurs that . . .

**chomped**

**hid**

**hopped**

stomped

and dinosaurs that . . .

...roared!

The dinosaurs **barged** through the trees with their very **pointy** spikes . . .

and **sped** across the forest with their very **fast** legs.

They **splashed** along the water
with their very **long** tails . . .

and **fished** among the swamps
with their very **sharp** claws.

Some dinosaurs laid **eggs** in a super-sized **nest**...

lined with **soft**,
sandy soil and green,
**springy** plants.

They waited for the eggs to **hatch** into . . .

. . . **teeny tiny** baby dinosaurs!

While in the sky . . .

. . . giant reptiles as big as planes **flew** through the air.

And down below

enormous sea beasts **swam** through the oceans.

**snap!**

Until the day arrived . . .

when the forest turned to **fire**
and the sky turned to **ash** . . .

and almost all the dinosaurs **died**.

They were **buried** by the earth

and the **sand**

and the **mud**

over **millions**
of years . . .

and their bones turned into fossils
buried **deep** underground.

While over time
**new** animals grew

who walked through the forest,

then **dug up**
the ground . . .

. . . and found the **bones** of a beautiful **beast** . . .

that lived on Earth millions of years ago.